BEING AN ACTIVE CITIZEN
VOLUNTEERING

by Vincent Alexander

pogo

Ideas for Parents and Teachers

Pogo Books let children practice reading informational text while introducing them to nonfiction features such as headings, labels, sidebars, maps, and diagrams, as well as a table of contents, glossary, and index.

Carefully leveled text with a strong photo match offers early fluent readers the support they need to succeed.

Before Reading

- "Walk" through the book and point out the various nonfiction features. Ask the student what purpose each feature serves.
- Look at the glossary together. Read and discuss the words.

Read the Book

- Have the child read the book independently.
- Invite him or her to list questions that arise from reading.

After Reading

- Discuss the child's questions. Talk about how he or she might find answers to those questions.
- Prompt the child to think more. Ask: Have you volunteered to help other people before? How did you feel about the experience?

Pogo Books are published by Jump!
5357 Penn Avenue South
Minneapolis, MN 55419
www.jumplibrary.com

Library of Congress Cataloging-in-Publication Data

Names: Alexander, Vincent, author.
Title: Volunteering / by Vincent Alexander.
Description: Minneapolis, MN : Jump!, [2018]
Series: Being an active citizen | Includes index.
Identifiers: LCCN 2018010707 (print)
LCCN 2018011811 (ebook)
ISBN 9781641280303 (ebook)
ISBN 9781641280280 (hardcover : alk. paper)
ISBN 9781641280297 (pbk.)
Subjects: LCSH: Voluntarism–Juvenile literature.
Volunteers–Juvenile literature.
Classification: LCC HN49.V64 (ebook)
LCC HN49.V64 A44 2019 (print) | DDC 302/.14–dc23
LC record available at https://lccn.loc.gov/2018010707

Editor: Kristine Spanier
Book Designer: Molly Ballanger

Photo Credits: asiseeit/iStock, cover; JEONGHYEON NOH/Shutterstock, 1; Africa Studio/Shutterstock, 3; Tassii/iStock, 4; Solis Images/Shutterstock, 5 (background); WaffOzzy/iStock, 5 (tablet); ZUMA Press, Inc./Alamy, 6-7; Steve Debenport/iStock, 8-9; Blend Images - Hill Street Studios/Getty, 10; Ariel Skelley/Getty, 11; fstop123/iStock, 12-13, 14, 18-19; Don Mason/Getty, 15; Diyana Dimitrova/Shutterstock, 16-17; Sappington Todd/Getty, 20-21; OlegDoroshin/Shutterstock, 23.

Printed in the United States of America at Corporate Graphics in North Mankato, Minnesota.

TABLE OF CONTENTS

CHAPTER 1

HELPING OUT

What does it mean to volunteer? It is offering help to someone who needs it. We don't expect money for our time. In fact, we don't expect anything in return at all.

Benjamin Franklin spread the idea of volunteering in the 1700s. He said we can work together to help one another. He started the first volunteer fire department. Franklin's ideas became a **foundation** of our **democracy**.

Benjamin Franklin

Some organizations send volunteers around the world. The American Red Cross is one. People need help after **disasters**. They may need **temporary** housing. They may need clothing, food, and clean drinking water. Volunteers help. We give our time. We use our skills. We may even give our own money to pay for what is needed.

DID YOU KNOW?

Volunteers do not get paid. But the work we do has great value. Across the United States, people provide more than 7.5 billion hours of service every year!

volunteer coach

Some people volunteer close to home. They work at schools. They help students with lessons. Or they coach teams. They referee games. Others volunteer to collect food for people who need it. Some may deliver meals to people who can't leave their homes.

We might know the people we are helping. Or we may never even see them. Volunteering is one way to be an active citizen.

CHAPTER 2
ACTIVE CITIZENS

Active citizens take part in our democracy. They **obey** laws. They serve on **juries**. They vote in elections.

Some serve in the military.

Disaster
Relief

Active citizens are involved in their **communities**. They identify problems. They ask questions. They create **solutions**. They work together to improve the lives of others. Volunteering is a duty that all active citizens can participate in. Your age doesn't matter.

WHAT DO YOU THINK?

How does it feel when you help people? Do you take pride in your work? Do you feel like you are contributing?

CHAPTER 3

GETTING STARTED

How do we start volunteering? Sometimes people ask for help. Other times we see a need we can help with and we jump in.

An easy place to start might be right next door. Do you have elderly neighbors? Offer to walk their dogs. Collect mail for them. Offer to help with lawn care or house projects.

Do you like to garden? Some people are not able to maintain a garden. Or they do not have the space. But they would like fresh fruits and vegetables. You can grow a garden for them at your own home. Or you can find space for a **community garden**.

WHAT DO YOU THINK?

Do you enjoy preparing food? Some **shelters** might need help making and serving meals. Who else would benefit from food that you can provide?

Collect spare change in a jar. When the jar gets heavy, exchange the coins for dollars at the bank. Give the money to your teacher. It can help pay for school supplies. Or field trips. Where else could you donate money?

TAKE A LOOK!

Individuals can make a difference. There are many places in your own community that could use your help!

ANIMAL SHELTERS
Collect blankets for cages. Make toys for the animals.

PARKS
Pick up litter. Play with kids who are alone.

FOOD SHELVES
Collect food donations from friends and neighbors.

SCHOOLS
What subjects are you really good at? Ask teachers if you can work with students who need help.

HOSPITALS
Collect used books to donate to patients. Fill clean shoeboxes with small games and puzzles for kids.

SENIOR CENTERS
Play cards with seniors. Have conversations with them. Ask them what life was like when they were young.

We **benefit** from our own volunteer work. We make new friends. We get to do something we enjoy. We learn new skills.

Many of us need help at some point in our lives. Today you can help others. Tomorrow they can help you. Together we can all be active citizens.

ACTIVITIES & TOOLS

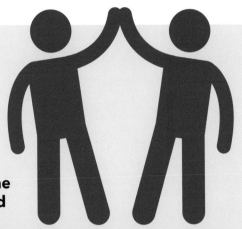

MANY HANDS CAN HELP

What do you do when you see a need for help but the job is too big for you? Put together a team! How?

1. Let your friends know about the problem. Ask who is interested in helping you with it.

2. Hold a meeting. Brainstorm ideas for how you can solve the problem. Vote on which idea is best.

3. Do you need supplies to make it happen? Where can you get them? Talk it over with one another. Can each person donate one item?

4. Decide when you will do the work. Choose a date. Make sure your parents or guardians know what you are doing.

5. Work together to complete your project! Was it a success? Does more work need to be done? Hold another meeting and decide what the next steps are.

GLOSSARY

benefit: To receive something that helps you.

communities: Places and the people who live in them.

community garden: A single piece of land gardened by and for a group of people.

democracy: A form of government in which the people choose their leaders in elections.

disasters: Events such as floods, earthquakes, or hurricanes that cause great damage or loss of life.

foundation: The basis of something.

juries: Groups of people who listen to the facts at trials and decide whether the accused person or people are innocent or guilty.

obey: To carry out or follow orders or instructions.

shelters: Places where homeless people, victims of disasters, or unwanted animals can stay.

solutions: Answers to problems.

temporary: Lasting for only a short time.

INDEX

TO LEARN MORE

Learning more is as easy as 1, 2, 3.

1) Go to www.factsurfer.com

2) Enter "volunteering" into the search box.

3) Click the "Surf" button to see a list of websites.

With factsurfer, finding more information is just a click away.